Diapers, Daycare, and Deadlines

SURVIVAL HACKS FOR SUPER BUSY PARENTS

Jan Cornell

Dedication

I dedicate this book to all the busy parents out there, who tirelessly dedicate their lives to their family and children.

To my village: Keith, Jack, Katie, Christina, Mark, Tammy, Pete, Buddy and Christi, Steve and Eva, John and Irene:

I love you all so much!

Terry: It was you who secured a proper diagnosis of Lyme Disease for me. Without your guidance, I likely would not be here today. Thank you!

Anne Zimanski: Thank you for being the most awesome, professional, talented, and creative illustrator ever!

Phil: Thank you for helping me complete this project. Your talent is incredible. We could not have done this without you!

To my friends across the country who believed in this journey: Katie A, Kim M, Angelique G, Jeanne C, Angela W, Christina R, Caiti B, Tamara G, Mark M, Phil M, Anne Z, Mabry R, Emily C, Theresa D, Amy RB, Diane D, Christine M, Terry A, Brooke W, Christina PM and Kristen C, Thank you!

Contents

Introduction

Several years ago I was pregnant, working, gravely ill, responsible for an active four-year old little boy, and had zero room for slouching on the motherhood job. During the almost year and a half that Lyme Disease ravaged my body undiagnosed, I learned how to do things around my home in a minimalistic approach with a twist of organization. In many ways my battle with Lyme Disease gave me the privilege of starting my life over, and allowed me to learn how to live life much more efficiently, and with more meaning and purpose.

During my learning process I would post various household and parenting hacks on social media. My friends across the country loved them. That was how this book was born.

Whether you are working one, two or even three jobs, shuffling a child around to doctor's appointments, dealing with illness yourself, or just plain busy, I promise these hacks will make your life so much easier. If you love just one of these hacks I will consider this project a success!

Set it Up

In order to master this busy parenting thing, you need to set your home environment up for success. Here are a few of my favorite hacks for setting up a chaos-free household.

Bulletin Boards

We have bulletin boards everywhere! These boards keep us organized and up to date with flyers and invitations. They also help serve as constant visual reminders. My kids enjoy seeing their current and prized artwork up on bulletin boards in their rooms.

Homemade Kindling

I don't recommend starting a fire around children; however, if you need to start a fire, dryer lint, empty paper towel holders, and paper shredder chips all make efficient and free kindling. We use this combo for our outdoor chiminea often.

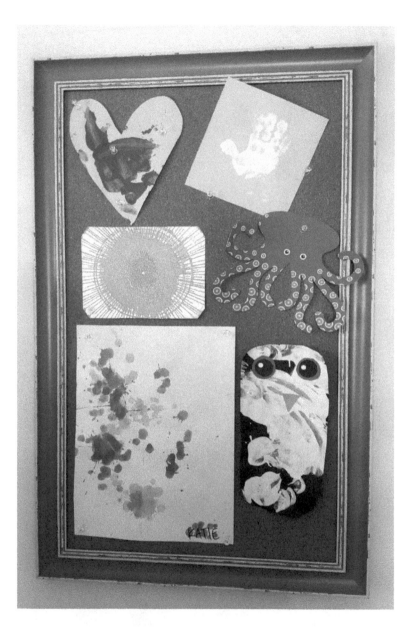

Beds with Drawers

No matter how big or small your home is, beds with drawer storage are amazing. They cost about the same as traditional beds and basically double storage space. We use bed drawers for the majority of our toy storage, clean up, and organization. My son Jack made a craft center out of one of his bed drawers where he and his sister play often!

We live in the Northeast, where space is extremely limited. Our master bedroom is on the smaller side so we use our master bed drawers to store everything from shoes, sweaters and boots to other various items. Beds with drawers also allow you to ditch outdated and high-maintenance bed skirts.

Outdoor Dining Ware for Indoors

A few years ago we switched out all of our indoor 'real' glassware to upscale outdoor durable plasticware. Outdoor plasticware is so advanced now that it looks just like the real thing. We now have no more broken glass and our drinkware lasts forever. Real glass and kids just do not mix!

We still use real plates occasionally; however, if you dine in our home you will likely be drinking from durable plastic drinkware. This hack will save you some serious headaches and aggravation. My kids used to break glasses on a weekly basis and it was becoming a safety hazard. It would also make for a terrible start to our workdays and weekends.

Retire Your Towels

We used to do insane amounts of laundry every single day. Both my husband and I felt extremely drained by our laundry burden. After putting our heads together, we determined that towels were the bulk of our laundry mess. We used to have a very nice towel closet in our bathroom that was readily overstocked with towels.

I packed up our entire towel closet with the exception of one towel for each of us and stored them away in our guest bed drawers. I had our names monogrammed on our remaining towels so we each received just one. I installed hooks in each bedroom on the backs of doors and in closets. Everyone in our home is in charge of their own towel now. If a towel ends up on the floor, I know who is responsible. This hack cut our laundry burden in half and was a complete life saver for our family. No more laundry madness!

Lazy Susan

We use Lazy Susans all over our home. They are perfect for crafting, serving food, and organizing. I buy them at The Salvation Army and Savers. The vintage ones are the best and most inexpensive.

Knives with Covers

Knives with covers are so much safer around kids, and extremely convenient for storing as well. No more bulky knife holder on the counter. We bought our set online for under $20.00.

Up-Cycle Grocery Bags

Occasionally I will not have reusable grocery bags with me and I will need to run an errand or make a stop. I always save small grocery bags and either put them in our recycling bin or re-purpose them as trash bags for our home and vehicles. I make the dispenser out of used and washed disposable wipe containers, and printable labels.

Create a Playroom

If space and funds allow, make a dedicated playroom for your kids. We live in a modest home and we were still able to make room for a playroom in our basement. It has a snack bar, a TV for movies and a chalkboard wall that our kids enjoy being creative with. Our playroom is nothing fancy but our kids absolutely love it. They write on both the walls and painted floors with chalk and have a ball.

Physical Calendars Everywhere

We keep calendars everywhere. When you are a busy parent, it's easy to lose track of time and even forget what day it is all together. I have a desktop calendar that I swear by and also use printed internet calendars. These are a great visual reminder of time.

Magnetic Catch-All Clip

Ours is on our refrigerator in our garage; however, if you have any metal doors in your house, these are ideal for metal doors. We use these clips for various notes and reminders.

Chalkboards!

We have two wall chalkboards in our home, and we use them every single day. I write festive seasonal greetings on our kitchen chalkboard, and our kids love practicing their art skills on the playroom chalkboard. We have been able to minimize holiday trinkets and clutter with simple holiday messages on both chalkboards.

Washable Dry Erase Markers

Working in the world of science, I can tell you one thing that most scientists have in common is they write all over everything with dry erase markers. I have seen researchers write on walls, windows, glass top desks, glass partitions, and even countertops. I started doing the same thing at home and nothing is off limits now.

We write notes, communications, and much more on windows, appliances, mirrors, and even toilets! Dry erase markers work really well for the workplace too. Mix up your meeting by writing on windows instead of the same ole dry erase board. All marks wipe right off with a tissue or dry cloth.

Garage Recreation Room

We cleared out our garage years ago and created extra living space. We painted the walls, ceiling, and floor to transform the space. Our new space has worked out well because we can run on the treadmill, and our kids can play when there is rain, snow or when it's dark outside. We also installed an almost second kitchen situation in our garage. This space used to be cluttered, gross, and useless. Now we all enjoy and utilize this excellent recreation room!

Be Emergency Ready

At any given time our household has stockpiles of homemade frozen dinners in our freezer and a stocked snack bar. No matter what your income you can always load up at the regular grocery store, wholesale stores, The Dollar Tree, food bank or your local food pantry. Food in your home should be your priority above all else. Lastly, there is a difference between stockpiling useful items and unhealthy hoarding habits. Hoarding is gross.

Ditch Your Linen Closet

Linen closets are outdated and not really necessary anymore. We have a small box of extra sheets in each bedroom closet, which is all we need. I have not had to fold any fitted sheets since I started doing this. I simply place the clean fitted sheet at the bottom of the extra sheet box, and it's done. Attempting to fold fitted sheets is a complete waste of life!

Secure Furniture

I always try to 'avoid the unavoidable.' Furniture tipping over on your children is totally avoidable. These tragic accidents happen all of the time. Simply anchor all bookcases, heavy and tippable furniture to the wall. This one hack could save a child's life. The following photo displays a set of IKEA book cases that we purchased for our home office. They are fully secured to the wall. All tippable furniture in our home is.

Hotel Home

Several years ago, a water pipe burst in our home, which caused significant damage. It took two months to fix our home, and during that time we lived at The Residence Inn in Middletown, Rhode Island. One thing I noticed about my family is how happy we were living in the hotel! Why in the world were we so glad? We were away from our home and all of our stuff. I thought at the time that we should have been super sad. It didn't make any sense at first. While The Residence Inn is a modest hotel, it is extremely clutter-free, clean, simple, and they host silly, cheesy games and events for kids on most nights. We only had about five outfits each so laundry was a breeze. The hotel would do a simple Taco Tuesdays or Salad Saturdays and as cheesy as it sounds my family loved it! I learned so much about myself and my family during that hotel stay.

After we finally moved back into our home, I vowed to bring that hotel feel back with us. We ended up doing some extreme simplifying, and we now treat our house like it's a fun hotel as well. Why would you only want to feel fresh, clutter-free and happy when you go away! I want my family to feel that way all the time! We started this journey a few years ago, and we have never looked back!

Pet Fish

It will happen. Your kids will ask for a fish. We have been down this road twice, and if you are truly a busy parent the fish will die, you will have spent a few hundred dollars, and endless hours of time setting everything up. I finally found a solution to this situation during a trip to a local museum. There is a company that sells small fake fish tanks, and they are epic! You will need a few rounds of batteries to keep your tank going long term. We have two versions and our friends and family always think they are real. We usually purchase these from a company called Warm Fuzzy Toys which has other great educational toys and gifts, too. These tanks make fantastic gifts, and they are extremely affordable.

Ice Trays with Covers

I could write an entire book on uses for ice trays with covers. We use ice trays to freeze liquids for smoothies, bone broth, and other homemade soups and sauces. My kids love it when we make ice tray buffets for road trips and other events. I usually stack a few of these trays already prepared in a small cooler and take them with us to the beach, on trips, picnics, and other outings. Family members of all ages love these treat trays. Ice trays with covers can also be used to store crafting supplies such as beads, gems, treasures from nature, and much more.

Dresser Drawer Storage

Dresser drawer space is prime real estate. If you can keep a minimalist size clothing collection, it is possible to fit all of your clothes in your closet. Condensing your clothes will leave dresser drawers wide open for storage. Dressers instantly become a toy box, craft center, or other storage medium.

Ditch Your Curtains

Curtains are outdated and also extremely high maintenance to take care of. You don't need them and they are old school and impractical anyway! A simple set of plastic or wood blinds does the job. Long curtains are also a safety issue for small children who tend to pull and swing on them.

Silverware Sorters

Silverware sorting trays are amazing to organize just about any small items. You can use them for office supplies, crafts, small toy pieces, make-up, toothbrushes, and more!

Winter Cubbies

Use a shoe holder with printable labels to store winter items. Ours is mounted to the back of our closet door which makes items readily available for kids.

You don't have to use this hack for just winter items. These pockets are useful for cleaning, laundry, office supplies, and whatever else your creative mind can come up with.

Paper Towel Holder Below Deck

Mount your paper towel holder onto one of your bottom kitchen cabinet doors so your kids can reach it. This will also clear valuable countertop space.

Direct Mail Catalog Decorating

Before I recycle catalogs, I always check out staging in catalog photos first. Catalog companies spend a lot of money hiring the best decorators in the world to produce their catalog photos. I always get my decorating ideas from junk mail

That said, I can't stand junk mail. I think it's a gigantic waste of natural resources. Junk mail should be outlawed. I have put myself on dozens of 'no not mail' lists for years and yet I still receive piles of junk mail catalogs. I use them to my advantage.

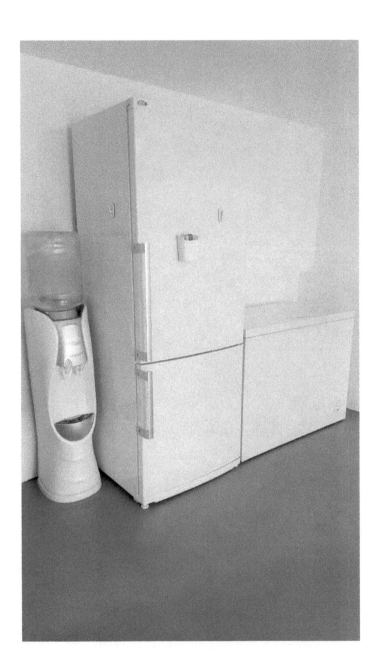

Back-Up Kitchen

Set up a back-up kitchen situation if you have a garage or any other extra space. We set up a mini second kitchen in our garage. We have water delivered, an extra refrigerator which was from our old kitchen and a chest freezer.

We use this fridge, freezer and water duo every single day. The extra fridge is great for storing birthday cakes, pre-cooked holiday food, beverages for company, and larger food items for holidays. In our deep freezer we are able to store cooler packs, dozens of homemade frozen dinners, and so much more. This was a game changer for our household!

Double Washer and Dryer

It is so nice to have two sets of washers and dryers. I do not have this installed in my current home; however, it is on my wish list. I have had this set up in the past, and it was wonderful. We are aiming to have two small stackable side by side units, sooner rather than later! Many spaces allow for two small stackable units, next to each other. Think mini laundromat, but in your own home.

Glass Tops

I have a glass top on my desk and on a few other pieces of furniture in our home. Glass tops allow you to display keepsakes and photos without taking up any other real estate within your home.

Backpack Hooks

We installed backpack hooks outside of both Jack and Katie's bedrooms. We used to misplace backpacks, and we would have to search all over the place for them. Not anymore! I know now exactly where to look for school folders, backpacks and lunch bags.

Paint Your Floors

I have owned three properties with painted floors. I know someone is thinking 'No way, that will kill the resale value.' Nope! I had zero issues selling any of the properties mentioned. One of my past properties was a condo that had carpet when I purchased it. I removed all the carpet myself hoping for hardwoods, but it was plywood! New floors were not in the budget, so I painted the all the plywood white. It looked awesome!

Painted floors are also great because kids can draw on them with washable markers and chalk, and clean-up is extremely easily.

Retire Your Iron

We stopped ironing a long time ago. I found it to be extremely dangerous to have a hot iron sitting on an ironing board with kids around. In addition to safety issues with irons, who in the world has the time?

I never purchase clothing for my family that needs to be ironed. Ironing is like trying to fold a fitted sheet, it's a waste of life. We own minimal suits and dress attire, and what we do own and use gets sent to the cleaners.

Avoid Carpet

Carpet is difficult to keep clean and is basically always filthy when children are involved. I would rather have painted plywood than carpet. Carpet can also make family members sick, especially if they are susceptible to allergies and respiratory infections. One round of your child vomiting it, and your carpet is toast. It's a bad investment.

Hooks by Each Door

Hooks placed by each door will ensure that jackets, umbrellas, and bags find a home off of the floor and do not get lost.

Trash Bag Garment Bags

I don't recommend moving with kids but, if necessary, unscented trash bags make great quick homemade garment bags. I have used small black kitchen trash bags in a pinch for various trips, both business and personal. No one knows the difference and who cares if they do!

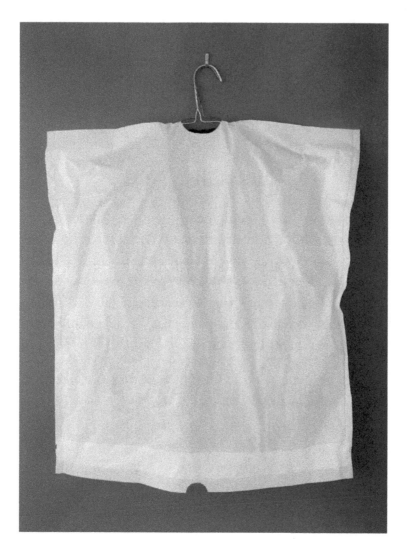

Minimalist Yard

We sold our lawn equipment to create space in our garage, and hired a lawn service. After comparing costs, it cost the same to pay a lawn service as it does to maintain all of our yard equipment. Now with the amount of ticks and Lyme Disease out there, I am so happy that we made this choice. We leave our yard maintenance to professionals now.

All of the plants and shrubs in our yard are minimal, hearty and easy to take care of.

Water Bottles

Everyone in our home has their own water bottle. This one hack has saved us so many loads of dishes it's not even funny. We wash these bottles regularly, which is obviously very important. Before we implemented this hack into our household, we had dozens of dirty cups and glasses all over our home, 24/7.

Let's Eat

If you want to be a rock star for your kids and family, you must get the 'let's eat' down! You and your family will all be miserable if there are never any prepared foods and readily available snacks in your home. Here are some of my favorite hacks around our favorite thing to do, EAT!

Cereal Necklace

These are super easy to make and are perfect for doctor appointments, trips, and all other outings! These necklaces keep kids occupied and happy!! Always supervise your child when they are wearing their necklace. I like to use stretchy necklace-making elastic from craft stores when making ours. Cereal necklaces do make a bit of a mess. Pass them out with caution!

Make a Snack Bar in Your Home

Our snack bar is the best thing that we ever created! My kids love their snack bar! A simple snack corner or snack bar will allow your kids to enjoy another part of your home and will keep both children and spouses out of the kitchen while you are trying to cook. When we have friends over for play dates, the first place my kids want to show them is the snack bar! Anyone can do this no matter what type of home you own. All you need is a spare wall or two and some simple shelving.

Make Your Own Frozen BP&J Squares

Make large amounts of homemade PB&J's packed full of organic peanut butter and jelly and freeze them. If you do not have a peanut allergy in your home these sandwiches are extremely convenient, inexpensive to make, and a huge hit with kids.

Pizza Cutter

Use a pizza cutter to cut simple things in your home like sandwiches, french toast, pancakes, chicken nuggets, cheeses, and many other foods. When my kids were both small, I hated having a knife out on our kitchen counter for safety reasons. We appreciate how simple, safe and convenient a pizza cutter can be with small children around.

Grow Your Own Food

Grow your own food if you can. We have two peach trees, chickens, and next summer I am starting a mega-garden. Growing your own food is so awesome. Gardening is a great activity for your entire family and it's a hobby that yields fruitful rewards.

Gardening and growing your own food is more work up front, however nothing is more convenient and healthy than picking fresh fruits and vegetables straight from your yard or patio. We have a deep freezer in our garage, and we try and freeze as much as we can so we can enjoy our fresh goodness year round.

Dinner Winner

This dinner tray will get even the pickiest of eaters to eat! Dinner Winner is an adorable game that gets kids to eat a string of food squares, and when they reach the end, they receive a prize whatever that may be. My son Jack is a highly picky eater, and I can easily get him to eat several full Dinner Winner trays in a row! My daughter Katie is not a picky eater, but she certainly goes crazy over our Dinner Winner trays too. These trays were invented in our home state of Rhode Island which makes them even neater!

Prep and Freeze

If I didn't do this, my life would be miserable! You name it - I cook it and freeze it when I have extra time. We always have a surplus of homemade healthy 'frozen dinners' on hand. Instead of meal planning I prep and freeze. We pull dinner out of the freezer on a nightly basis. In order to be successful at this, I have had to give up a few time wasters. The reward has been a very happy family! I have actually come to enjoy doing this; likely because of how easy it makes our life!

In addition to prepping and freezing, while I am in the kitchen I will bag snacks. I buy my snack bags at The Dollar Tree and while waiting for things to cook, bake, and cool, I pre-bag. I use these snacks to fill lunches, activity bags, vehicle snack boxes, and our snack bar. The goal is that when you are in the grind and pressed for time, all food prep is already done.

Protein Shakes

I have never met a picky eater that will refuse a chocolate milkshake. Load shakes with banana, almond milk, and a spoonful of almond butter. Sometimes that is just what everyone is in the mood for, and it's a relatively easy snack to make! If your child takes probiotics or liquid vitamins, protein shakes are an excellent way to get them to take their vitamins. Protein shakes are a win-win for everyone.

Fresh Fruit

Mount an office organizer to the side of your kitchen cabinet or inside your pantry. If you mount it low, this allows kids to help themselves to an apple or banana. Both of our kids love this! Always wash all fruit before we put it away because kids will not remember to do so.

Save Containers

We enjoy ordering take-out every once in a while. If our take-out arrives in a nice plastic container, we always wash it and reuse it for lunches, or for making homemade frozen dinners. Occasionally groceries are packaged in useful containers which we also wash and save. We do not hoard. We save what we will use; there is a difference! One of our favorite grocery store reusable containers is the plastic egg holder. I wash plastic egg crates with soap and hot water, and we use them for dozens of projects around our home, especially painting and crafts.

Measuring Spoon Melon Baller

Measuring spoons make perfect melon ballers in a pinch.

Cold Bottles

Not every baby will go for this but my daughter loved drinking her bottles cold or room temperature. My son on the other hand, his bottles had to be a certain temperature, not too hot, not too cold, which was difficult to achieve at times. If your child doesn't have a preference for milk temperature, then go with the straight-from-the-fridge option! My daughter would drink her cold bottle and go right back to sleep.

Dinner Basket

Keep a box on your dinner table that includes a collection of disposable eating supplies. I have been doing this since I was pregnant with my son, and was working very long hours in Corporate America. We always buy all the most eco and earth friendly products and brands. I used a dinner box when I brought both of my babies home from the hospital. It's a game changer.

We don't use our dinner box all the time; however during times of chaos, struggle, or extreme busyness, it's truly a life saver! This hack also keeps germ spreading at bay during flu and stomach bug outbreaks.

Pu Pu Platter

There is nothing that my family loves more than a homemade Pu Pu platter. I put a bunch of random items in a veggie serving platter with dividers, and my entire family enjoys it. I find most of our veggie serving pieces at thrift stores. You can also put a Pu Pu Platter on a Lazy Susan, and your family will have so much fun with it.

Whatever food I throw into our Pu Pu Platter always becomes magically desirable and appealing to my family! Leftovers, random food, whatever you have, throw it in the Pu Pu Platter. You can also do different theme nights with veggie servers. Our favorite themes are tacos, hamburgers, hot dogs and salads.

It used to seem like no matter what we made for dinner, someone always wanted 'something else.' Our Pu Pu Platters totally solved that problem. There is something for everyone now.

Breakfast for Dinner

Breakfast is great any time of the day! If your kids are in an eating funk, usually a breakfast meal will perk things right up! Breakfast foods are also quick and easy to make on the fly.

Pizza

Occasionally we will order a pizza as a special treat. When ordering pizza, I either order the monster size with a coupon if I feel like packing and freezing, or I will purchase two individual size minis for our kids. Our kids love mini personal sizes, which are also dirt cheap. If Keith and I do not feel like splurging calories, we will go this route because it leaves little left over for splurging! We can usually purchase each child their own tiny pizza for under $10.00 total. When we purchase a monster size and freeze it, it makes life extremely convenient because both of our kids like cold pizza in their lunches.

Slow Cooker

We try to use a slow cooker twice a week. I used to cook in an extra-large slow cooker but I loathed it because it was a beast to handle and clean. It was just too much.

I found a mini slow cooker, and now I slow cook much more frequently. Although it does not cook in bulk sizes like my previous slow cooker, there always seems to be leftovers to freeze for later. Our smaller mini slow cooker is perfect to throw something random in like a side dish for dinner. Keep in mind cooking times will change in smaller sized slow cookers.

Snack Baskets

Have pre-bagged snacks ready in your pantry. We store snacks lower so our kids may help themselves. We also have our fully stocked snack bar downstairs.

Celebrate

Celebrating all the small occasions in life is simply the best. There is a big difference between celebrating pre-children and post-children. You now have triple the number of things to celebrate, in half the amount of time! Something has to give when trying to make it all work.

Celebrate

Wrap it Inside Out

All you need is a ball of twine and any roll of wrapping paper, and you can wrap anything, at any time! Who knows what wrapping paper our recipient will find on the inside of their gift! We do this for all holidays and special occasions because it is super simple and convenient. No more trying to match wrapping paper with an occasion.

Fake Out Your Tree

If you celebrate Christmas with a tree, purchase a fake one. We have one tree, with one set of simple decorations. All of our decorations fit in one extra-large box. I like the fact that we have the luxury of pulling out our tree and decorations at any point during the holiday season. There is no rushing around or cutting down trees. Fake holiday trees are also fantastic for those with allergies or allergy-prone children. Real Christmas trees also have the potential to bring bugs into your home. The thought of that totally grosses me out!

Holiday Cards

I vowed this year that I am done forever with large holiday card mailings. They are not always necessary and are also a gigantic waste of time and resources, especially when we have social media now. Getting my kids to take a family photo is a nightmare. The whole card situation is a nightmare! No more. We have switched to sending a very limited about of snail mail holiday cards out. I have also switched to emails and electronic invitations for birthday parties and all other gatherings. Everyone has an email address.

Baptize

Both of my kids were walking and talking by the time they were baptized. I think they were both around a year and a half old. Don't beat yourself up for not getting your kids baptized when you think you're supposed to. Do what works for you and your family.

After giving birth both times, there was no way I was up for planning a family get-together and baptism for a while. It was at least one year before I was ready to entertain after both childbirths. Go easy on yourself.

Birthday Lunch

Wrap a lunch surprise for your child on their birthday and put it in their lunch bag. I usually wrap two small cookies or something to that effect for birthday lunches. My kids always look forward to their special lunch treat on birthdays!

Buy Like Gifts

Giving 'like' gifts makes things incredibly easier on special occasions and holidays. If one child gets an item, so does the other. For example, if my son gets a sweater then so does my daughter. Likewise, if my daughter gets a sports type item then so does my son. If I keep things balanced, then it makes things easier on me and no one ever feels left out. There are exceptions to this rule; however, we try and stick with like gifts whenever we can.

Use Electronic Invitations

There is no need to waste money on paper birthday invitations. I think it's weird when someone sends a paper invitation unless it's for a wedding or formal event. Paper invitations are a gigantic waste of effort and natural resources.

Pot Luck Parties

If you feel the need to host a party, as long as it is not a formal event or a birthday party, make it a pot luck party. Many people are too proud to ask for help, or too embarrassed to request that guests bring a dish to their party. I love pot luck parties. I love hosting them and attending them. It's fun to try others creations and it's equally as enjoyable to show off your very own!

Appreciation Basket

During holidays I keep an appreciation basket handy instead of individualized gifts. In my basket is usually a wide range of prewrapped and inexpensive gifts. For special occasions I let my 'village' pick a gift out of the appreciation basket. They may choose a $10.00 coffee shop card or a $5.00 bill. The point is that everyone gets something and nothing is predetermined, so there is an element of fairness and surprise. Putting together this basket might sound like a lot of work, but it's much easier than trying to figure out individual gifts. Honestly, people love this. You can get as creative as you want with your baskets!

You can introduce this tradition to church friends, neighbors, school teachers, and anyone else that plays a role in your life throughout the year. This hack is also great if you work in a large office. An appreciation basket is a perfect way to show colleagues how much you appreciate their daily efforts. The following photo shows one of my Easter-themed appreciation baskets.

Family Stationery

Order or make your own family stationery and use it for every single card that you need, when you need to send a card. I use our cards for birthday party gifts and any other special occasions that we attend.

We usually have our kids color and decorate outgoing cards, which adds a personal and happy touch. I haven't bought an actual greeting card in a long time. Put a twine ribbon around your envelope for an elegant touch if there is a gift card or money inside.

Halloween Candy

We automatically freeze holiday candy after we let our children indulge for a day or two. It usually lasts until summer in our deep freezer. You can use this candy for special baking projects and even crafts for many months after Halloween.

BYOC to Birthday Parties

If your child has a food allergy, pre-make, freeze, and have a stockpile of allergy-free cupcakes ready to go at all times.

My girlfriend does this with her son, and it has helped ease the burden of his peanut allergy alongside allowing him to participate in the cake segment of birthday parties. My girlfriend uses disposable coffee cup containers with lids so she can freeze cupcakes individually and be able to transport them with ease. When it is time for her son to have his cupcake they simply cut off the cup wrapper and put it in recycling.

This hack works for all food allergy children. You can create your own tradition for your child according to their needs. You might make small frozen organic gummy cups if your child has a dairy allergy.

Surprise Box of Chocolates

Up-cycle chocolate box trays and fill them with something fun. I put all kinds of treats in recycled chocolate boxes. I use this hack for adults too. You can get as crazy as you want with this hack.

Surprise Drawer

I started a random drawer where I keep extra goodies, party favors, extra gifts that we receive, kid's meal toys, lollipops and other fun surprises that our family collects during our travels. Our surprise drawer is a great reward motivator for our kids.

Plan Ahead

Plan ahead financially and logistically for all celebrations. If you know your family is having a get together six months from now, start planning as soon as you can! If you can bite off a few teeny little tasks, before you know it, you will be ready for your party.

If I stop into a store and see something that would be good for an upcoming party, I will grab it then. I do not purchase items in advance to hoard them; I simply buy what I think we will need on a very minimalistic level. Overall I suggest keeping parties simple.

Special Letters

Letters from Santa and the Tooth Fairy can be overwhelming at times, especially if you have more than one child. I always either type something up quickly on my computer with a funky font, or I will write a note somewhere in our home on a wipeable surface with a dry erase marker. Bedroom windows are a great spot for Tooth Fairy and Santa notes.

Auto Bank Draft

I opened a separate bank account dedicated to Christmas and holiday savings. I have a very small amount automatically drafted from our family bank account every week.

My husband loves it when I reintroduce holiday shopping money every December. No matter what holidays you and your family celebrate, these funds always come in handy! Whatever you can spare to set aside, it's worth it!

Housekeeping

It's a never-ending story! How in the world are we ever supposed to keep everything tidy when we are so busy? It's a challenge, to say the least. I have spent several years trying to get the right cleaning routine down. At this point, everything is down to a science. Here are my best hacks to help you keep your kingdom tidy, too!

Less Stuff = Less Mess

It's that simple. It took me a long time to figure this out but less stuff = less mess. This one hack has changed our entire lives. Every single person that picks up this book could likely stand to get rid of half or more of their stuff. Old clothes, trinkets, outdated electronics, abandoned toys, you don't need any of it! When you have less stuff you will feel so much better, and you will also likely have extra time and money. Sell it, donate it and get rid of it, all of it!

Chaos Cleaning Steps

There will be times in parenting that your home looks like a hurricane hit it. Here are three simple cleaning steps to get your house under control quickly.

1. Trash, Recycling, and Donations – all of it!
2. Dishes
3. Laundry

After doing the above steps you can pick up where you usually do; however, the daunting bulk of the mess should be taken care of.

Disposable Toilet Wand

We use a disposable, biodegradable cleaning pad that sticks to the end of a wand. These pads can be released right into your trash can from your wand. Disposable wand pads are much more sanitary than having a dirty toilet bowl brush sitting around, especially if you have small children.

Wash It

If I am not able to wash something, it does not come into our home. Everything in our home gets cleaned on a regular basis. I wash sheets, comforters, furniture slip covers, floors, sneakers, jackets, clothing, dish sponges, and everything else in our home on a regular basis.

Automate Your Air Freshener

We use battery-powered air fresheners that spray automatically. Ours spray once or twice a day, and it's fantastic. It's like having a free assistant spray air freshener in your home.

Microwave Your Dish Sponge

Throw your dish sponge in the microwave for roughly fifteen seconds to sanitize and cook off any funky smells.

Robot Vacuum

We used to have a robot vacuum cleaner that I found new and in the box at a thrift shop. It was the best thing since sliced bread. It eventually broke, and we never replaced it. A robot vacuum is like having a free assistant to do your floors daily for you! I hope to get a new one soon.

White Vinegar

Add a splash of white vinegar in your laundry loads to make clothes smell fresh again. White vinegar is also perfect for cleaning tile floors, and many other hard surfaces. Using diluted white vinegar for cleaning will save you money and also spare your family from harsh chemicals.

Sweep It

Instead of using a vacuum on your hard surfaces, use a broom. I used to break vacuum cleaners once a year by vacuuming up a tiny toy or something of that nature. I ditched our push vacuum and opted for a hand held, and light-weight portable vacuum to pick up my sweep piles. Sweeping is much more convenient with kids because it's quiet and you can do it while they sleep. Many kids are terrified of larger, louder push vacuums.

Return Everything

If anything comes into your house that you don't like, return it. Don't let junk pile up in your house. Unwanted gifts, bad purchases, impulse buys, get rid of it all. If you are unable to return it, then sell or donate it. If I have too much stuff around me, it messes up my mojo.

Ditch Real Pens and Markers

Nothing is worse than a two-year-old getting a hold of a permanent pen or marker. We confiscated all permanent pens and markers in our home once our kids were mobile. Everything is now washable something or other.

Goo Gone and Goof Off

At two years old my daughter found a pen in my work bag, and she drew all over our white leather couch. Luckily for me, I was able to get the ink off the couch with Goo Gone. I love both Goo Gone and Goof Off for big-time oopsie disasters. Both Goo Gone and Goof Off should both be kept out of your child's reach.

Save Paint Can Lids

Save just your paint can lid, instead of an entire empty can of paint. Label it, stack it with the rest, and, voila, you have a portfolio of your home colors.

Washable Everything

Purchase only things that are washable and wipeable. We have washable slip covers on our furniture, or leather which is wipeable. A non-washable piece of furniture does not stand a chance against a stomach bug outbreak in your home.

Recycle Backpacks & Diaper Bags for Storage

Keep all of your kid's old backpacks and use them as time capsules. Most of our bags are monogrammed or have sentimental value and memories attached, which makes them perfect time capsules. We do not hoard keepsakes; however, it is important to keep some items for kids to look back on when they are older!

Disinfect with your Dishwasher

Occasionally I will do an entire load of non-battery operated toys in our dish washer. Your dishwasher is made to disinfect, take advantage of it! We wash many non-dish related items in our dishwasher.

Use Consignment Store Services

Drop off loads of junk that you no longer use at consignment stores. Consigning is extremely convenient, and we end up making extra activity money for our household.

Yes or No Method

When deciding what stays or goes in your home, it's either a yes or no. If you think about it for too long, you will never be able to get rid of anything. Do you love it? Do your kids love it? Yes or no?

Sock Buckets

I use repurposed laundry pod containers with printed labels to sort socks. Keith mounted a shelf right above our washer and dryer, and I sort our socks directly into pod buckets. Everyone in our home helps put their own socks away, after they are sorted into their pod.

If your pods fill up and you are extremely back logged with socks, an extra-large bucket with rope handles works well as a sock holding pen. During times of busyness I use our big bucket and let everyone fetch their own clean socks. We bought our bucket from a hardware store.

Hire Your Kids

Kids of all ages can help contribute to household chores. Find age-appropriate chores for your kids and pay them a fair amount to help out. Our son is just seven years old, and he can pick up his room, put away groceries, and set the table. Hiring your kids for even the smallest tasks is both a huge help and a win-win for all.

Bathroom Cleaning

I always save bathroom cleaning for right before I am about to take a shower. I scrub the bathroom first then take a hot shower. This bathroom cleaning method is the most sanitary, works out well and is extremely convenient.

Limit Toys

We limit toys. Limiting toys helps dramatically with mess. Our kids can fill up their dressers and bed drawers with toys, and after all those spots are filled, no more toys. Our kids have to donate an item to acquire an item if toy storage is at capacity. You have to set a limit.

Baby Wipes

We purchase fragrance-free baby wipes by the case for our house. We keep them in strategic locations around our home and our cars. Baby wipes are so incredibly handy for spills, cuts and scrapes, lunches on the go, and other messes.

Pre-Treat Laundry

I always have a reserve of stain remover in our laundry room. Pre-treat everything and let it sit.

White Vinegar/Dish Soap Combo

Mix equal parts of dishwashing soap and white vinegar for the most fantastic bathroom cleaner ever. I clean tubs, showers, sinks, and toilet bowls with this concoction. We avoid using harsh cleaning products in our home. This combo cleaner will get your bath tub literally squeaky clean with minimal scrubbing and effort.

Wash Your Small Toys

Wash small plastic toys in your washing machine in a delicate item mesh bag. This works for small figurines, and small building blocks.

Purge Boxes

We have four boxes set up in our garage. These boxes help keep our home organized and tidy and also help keep household overflow at bay. We have two boxes for recycling overflow, a donations box, and a junk mail burn or shred box.

Laundry Sorting

Sort laundry loads by room and family member, not by color. It works. Somehow our laundry makes it through the entire process with this method.

Permanent Marker Touch Ups

I keep a hidden collection of different colored permanent markers and touch up everything in our home with them. I touch up anything from scuffs on furniture, clothing, shoes, toys and even our hardwood floors. I mean you never really know what your kids are going to destroy next right? I have also used exact match wall paint as a last ditch option in many catastrophic stain situations - works every time. I have done this with furniture, car interiors, clothing and more.

On the Road

While on the road, you can prevent both boredom and disaster with your kids. If you prepare ahead of time, being on the road with your kids can actually be enjoyable!

Car Snack Bucket

My kids dig into our vehicle snack bucket every single day. If I ever took the snack bucket out of my car, my kids would be very upset! I make our vehicle snack buckets out of washed laundry pod buckets. I run them through the dishwasher then put a printable label on the front, and then simply fill with snacks.

Foldable Wagon

I keep a foldable wagon in my car. Our wagon is extremely convenient especially when it is warmer outside. Both of our kids love piling in, and going for a ride. I take them everywhere in it! We also use our wagon to put coolers and other items in while on family outings! Our wagon is like having a personal assistant!

Funzie Travel Wallet

Make travel funzie wallets for your kids. Fill them with stickers, colored paper, and other goodies to stay occupied. Funzie wallets work perfectly for church service, weddings and other moments where kids must sit still. Refill funzie wallets with fresh items for new adventures. You can make funzie wallets out of old retired adult wallets or newer children's versions.

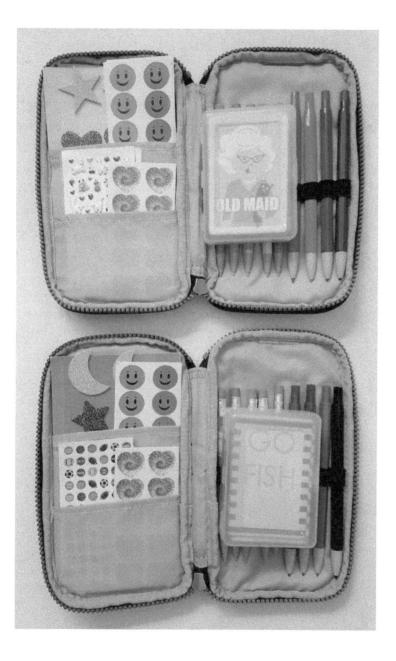

Vehicle Supply Kit

I have lost count of how many times my car has been thrown up, peed and pooped in. Keith and I both keep kits with emergency supplies in our cars. Our kits include a towel, an extra change of clothes for both of our kids, hand sanitizer, baby wipes, extra diapers, and travel sized toiletries. When something crazy happens it always seems to happen while we are driving in the car, so we have learned the hard way that it's best to be prepared at all times.

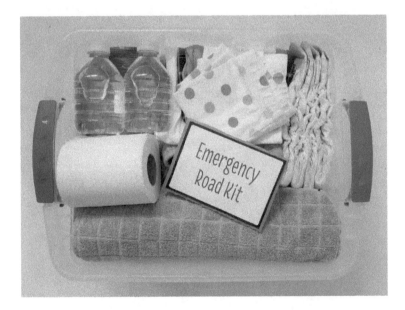

Travel Light

Be prepared but also travel light. The less stuff you have to lug around, the better. A lighter load will make you feel less stressed and overwhelmed, and you will enjoy your travels more. I always pack light and wash items while away for both myself and my family.

Windshield Trick

There is nothing worse than running out of windshield wiper fluid while driving in snow. Snowballs are the perfect solution if your windshield is not visible due to salt and muddy snow kickback. If you run out of wiper fluid, pull over in a safe place. After you pull over, turn your windshield wipers on low and toss a few snowballs at your windshield. The water from the snowballs will clear things up and allow you to see clearly for the rest of your journey.

The Grind

Our day-in and day-out grind can sometimes feel impossible to manage! Here are a few hacks that have made our crazy grind a little bit easier and less stressful!

Break it Down

Break down huge tasks into smaller, more manageable ones. I love painting and updating rooms in my house. I do not have the time to paint entire rooms all at once, so I paint one wall at a time. This method works very well, every time. When I was writing this book, I would write a few pages at a time. It worked. It always works!

Double Diaper

If you have a child who is always leaking through their diaper at night and waking up the whole house, try doing the double diaper method. When you put your child to bed put a diaper on them in their regular size, then put an extra diaper one size up on top to catch leaking. Double diapering will at least allow everyone to sleep through the night. This hack is also extremely helpful for stomach viruses and diarrhea. Oh, fun right?

Flexibility

If you work outside the home, aim for a flexible schedule. I have always worked in sales and have found that 'field-based sales' is a great job for Moms. Everyone can sell something. Working in a 'field-based home office' capacity allows you to work around your kids' schedules.

I usually follow a 50/50 rule when working from home. I work 50% on family requirements and 50% on work requirements. Every few hours I will switch gears. 50/50 is a target percentage that I strive for; however, my time always ends up balancing out in favor of my family. Sometimes I will work three days straight and get a mountain of work done, and then I will spend three days with my kids. As long as all of your work is completed, it doesn't matter when you get it done. Telecommute if you can.

Family Mailboxes

We each have an individual mailbox in our home office. My son Jack loves putting everyone's mail away in their mailbox. Our mailboxes are a great central location to leave items for each other such as notes and other important items.

Spa Day at Home

When your extremely busy and worn down, try to do a 'spa day' at home to relax. I buy cheapo spa products such as bubble bath, face masks, and other spa products and have a home spa day.

It would be very difficult to squeeze in a 'real' spa day with all of my obligations; however I can always do a spa evening, spa morning, or spa day right in the comfort of my own home and, at my own convenience.

Recalculate Your Worth

We all forget just how valuable that our time is. I play a game with myself where I pretend that I charge $1,000 per hour for my time. I have found that since I started playing this game I do not let others waste and drain my time like I used too. My time is extremely valuable. We can never get back lost time! Say yes to very little.

Layer Sheets

If you have a sick child you can always layer protective sheets so you don't have to change a full bed of sheets, in the middle of the night. Layer two full sets of sheets, wet protector and all. When your child has an accident you simply peel off the top layer and throw it in the laundry, and there is still another entire layer of sheets on the bed. You don't have to start a whole bed changing project at 1:00am anymore!

Lower Overhead

We keep our overhead low. The more overhead that you have, the harder you have to grind, no thank you! Live in the smallest space you and your family can stand, with the least amount of bills possible. Eliminate what you do not use. It's usually a yes or no, do you need it or not?

The two biggest bill splurges in our home that we technically do not 'need' are our water delivery service and our cable. Keith loves cable, and I love our water service, fair enough! Cancel every single service, subscription, and bill that you do not need and can live without. Lowering your overhead will allow you to work less and hopefully get ahead.

Alarms

Set alarms, lots of them. I use my kitchen alarm and my phone alarm. If you have to head to the bus stop in an hour and you're working or cleaning, set an alarm to remind yourself. If you give your kids a time allotment for a particular reason, mean it. Set your timer!

School Keeper Baskets

Our kids each have a basket for school work 'keepers.' Keep these baskets somewhere convenient and put all school keepers in them. These baskets or boxes can be emptied once per year. I usually put the content of each basket into each child's backpack for that year and then put it in the attic.

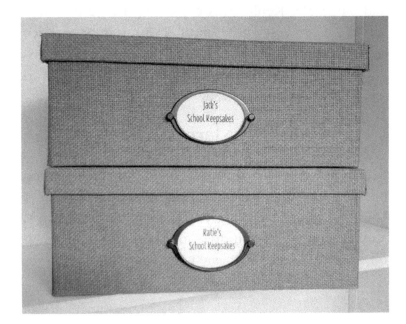

Be the Same Person

If you would never snip at a coworker while working, then don't do it at home. Why are we so polite at work, then come home and snip at our spouse or kids? Wear the same face in all places that you go. Seriously!

One 'to do' & One 'to clean'

Even if you feel super overwhelmed you can always do one 'to do' and one 'to clean' per day. My girlfriend who lives in Manhattan does this. She is a busy working Mom, and this helps her stay on top of things.

Delete

While sitting with any free idol time, delete items on your phone. It stresses me out when my phone has text, pictures, and email that are all exploding at the seams. I clean out my phone while I am sitting in meetings, on conference calls, waiting for appointments, and while traveling. Half of my cell phone photos are usually trash and need to be purged. You will thank yourself if you get in the habit of doing this.

Happiest Baby on the Block

Every new Mom needs this book, which also comes on video. I learned a tremendous amount as a new Mom by watching the video version. You will learn how to help a baby stop crying in just seconds, and it works like magic. *Happiest Baby on the Block* is by Harvey Karp, and is a must do for new parents. Best book ever, it saved my entry into motherhood!

Total Money Makeover

If you are having problems making ends meet, which many busy parents do, find Dave Ramsey and his ministry. Dave Ramsey hosts several national talk shows on behalf of his ministry and will teach you everything you need to know about money.

I found Dave and his book *Total Money Makeover* when I was in my 20's and attending college. I think I would be living in a cardboard box if it weren't for Dave, his daughter Rachel Cruz and their fantastic financial ministry! Dave and Rachel roll out real financial advice for real people in real situations, good and bad. If you have the opportunity to see this duo live, I highly recommend the experience! It was absolutely life changing for me.

123 Magic

This is the greatest book ever for discipline. If your child is misbehaving and not listening, *123 Magic* provides a gentle approach that works every time. When I first found this book, I wished that someone would have given me a copy or recommended it to me much sooner. This book truly lives up to its name. It works just like magic. Better late than never! *123 Magic* is by Thomas W. Phelan

Prayer Books

I keep several small children's prayer books on our kitchen table to remind us to say our prayers. Our kids enjoy this tradition and it reminds us to be thankful even when we are rushed and hurried at times. Our prayer books are all ultra-modern and relevant to today's times.

Make Everything a Contest

Our kids enjoy contests, so I roll them out often. Everybody loves a fun, fair, and motivating contest.

Homework Table

Create a homework table for your kids. I have a small table from IKEA in front of my home office desk. Our kids use it often for crafts, and homework. It's extremely convenient because I can pay bills or check email while they are doing homework, and I am right there to assist if needed. We all still get to spend time together even though we are doing our own thing, which is great!

Pay Bills Online

It took me a while to transfer to online bill pay. Wow does it make things easier. Set auto bill pay on as many bills as you are able. Having bills paid automatically is another free assistant.

Checkbook Binder

We used to have check books all over the place. Keith had one in his car, I had one in my car, we had a few sitting around our house, sound familiar? I finally ordered a thick checkbook binder and now we have one check book that stays in one place, and because of the recording ledgers, we know what checks have been written to whom, and when. We also do not run out of checks as often because check binders are much bigger than smaller more traditional checkbooks. We pay most things online; however, there is still a need for paper checks, especially for school fundraisers and events.

Stop Searching

Every morning we used to search around for routine items like a bunch of nuts. We could never find our hairbrushes, keys, wallets or cell phones. I ended buying several dozen hairbrushes, scissors, and other key items to stop the chaos. Keith and I also now have designated spots for our phones, wallet, keys, and other items. If there is an item that you are constantly going crazy looking for, go online and order a few of them to save your sanity.

Daily Timeline 'To Do'

If you have a to-do list for your day, try and arrange the items in order, by time. I usually group items by am and pm tasks.

Do Everything the Night Before

We do everything the night before. Doing this ensures our mornings run smoothly! We prepare lunches, homework, school projects, breakfast, outfits, snacks, and more the night before. Everyone leaves our home for the day feeling relaxed and happy! If we do not do this one hack, our days start off miserably.

Family Meetings

Just like you would request a meeting at work to discuss important issues, call a meeting at home to discuss matters as well. Quick family meetings can be a good time to discuss any new and exciting family news and are also an opportunity to talk about family expectations. Your children will always remember family meetings and becoming familiar with the process will also prepare your kids for the real world.

Treat Yourself

Every once in a while I will get a pedicure while I'm out or I will have an ice cream or something fun. You have to do this. We all work so hard for our kids, live it up a little if you can. One of my favorite indulgences is tacos. I will check out of life and order a big ole bag of tacos with hot sauce and have a ball. The best! Whatever 'your thing' is, do it!

Dim the Lights

Dim your lights at dinner time to encourage your kids to calm down. Our kids will usually settle a bit after I dim the lights. This makes for an easier transition into bedtime.

Extra Jobs

Anything extra that you choose to be involved in is essentially an extra job. I used to max myself out all the time with tons of extra 'jobs.' I am not Superwoman, and I cannot be in ten different places at once! Before you agree to an additional project or volunteer for extra duties, just remember how many 'jobs' you are already juggling. It all adds up very quickly.

For Divorced Parents

Make sure you and your ex each have a duplicate set of everything. If you attempt to 'share' certain things such as soccer equipment and other items, you will both end up extremely frustrated. The constant run around and meeting up to exchange items is unnecessary and exhausting. Keep a full set of belongings at both homes to eliminate possible conflict and frustration.

'To Do' Buckets

Make a set of 'to do' buckets for your kids. These buckets will allow your children to track progress during the busy hustle of mornings and evenings. I usually give out decent privileges and rewards if all tasks are completed without nagging or bickering.

Open Drain Baths

I rarely shut the drain while my kids are in the tub. Both my kids love sitting in an empty tub while it's 'raining'! They play and have a ball, and I don't have to worry about standing water. This option is much safer than the alternative. This hack doesn't apply to my seven year old who takes regular showers now.

Crazy Day

When there is 'crazy day' at any of our schools we all usually remember that morning. At the beginning of the school year I usually make sure both of my children each have:

1. A crazy hat
2. A crazy pair of socks
3. A pair of pajamas suitable for school
4. A sports jersey
5. Items for crazy hair day

You will thank yourself if you prepare for these special days ahead of time!

Word Bracelets

Word bracelets are so much fun and have many different uses. You can find word bracelet kits at most craft stores. With your kit you can -

1. Make Allergy Alert bracelets for your kids.
2. Use them to remind yourself of something important.
3. Relay messages for non-verbal kids such as, 'I don't like milk.'
4. Use them to help your kids learn new words over the summer.
5. Make a bracelet with your phone number for your child.

Preprinted School Notes

Have a stack of preprinted school notes for your kids ready to go. I loathe writing notes for school on the fly. The easier you can make the process the better. You can make your own preprinted notes, or order custom notepads online.

Preprinted school notes can also include special reminders at the bottom such as 'Please remember that Parker has a peanut allergy, thank you!'

a note from the mom of

☐ Jack   ☐ Katie

Jan Cornell
401.808.9800
jancornell711@gmail.com

Letters as I Watch You Grow

I love these journals that I am creating for my kids. I ordered these journals online and occasionally will leave a note or printed and trimmed internet quote in them. I can't wait to give these to my kids someday. They will make an amazing graduation or wedding gift.

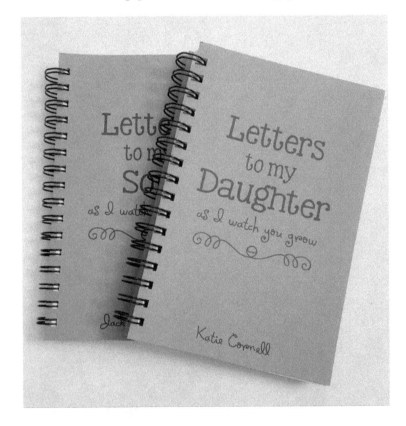

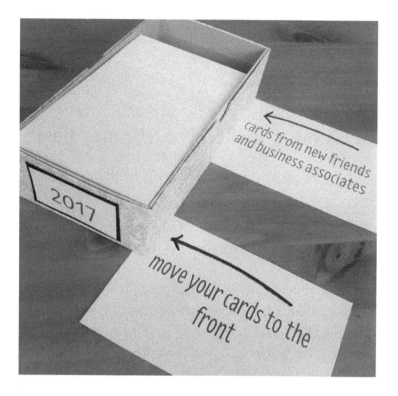

Business Cards

When I order new business cards, I use the original box for storing incoming and outgoing cards. I used to purchase bulky card holders and other nonsense to store business cards. Now I just rotate cards through the lovely original box, and when it is full it serves as storage for contacts made that year.

Set Your Clocks Five Minutes Fast

Works every single day of my life!

Pre-Make Baby Supply Kits

These kits are meant to be snatched in a hurry to re-stock your diaper bag. If you choose to take your family out on the fly, you don't want to have to stop everything and repack baby supplies. We used these filler kits often when our kids were little. These are also perfect for Grandparents picking up kiddos last minute!

All you need to make these kits are large disposable plastic bags, diapers, wipes, and any other necessities that are unique to your family. Pre-make a dozen of these and have them on hand at all times. Make sure to restock your kits as you use them.

Eliminate Time Wasters

There are many different activities that we can all agree waste gigantic amounts of time. These activities need to be eliminated in order to provide your kids with the life that they deserve. What are your big time wasters?

Wake Up Ready

Have your kids get fully ready the night before you have an early morning. Let them sleep in comfy soft sweat suits and socks, so all they have to do is put their shoes on. This also works for children who act out in the morning. You don't need to do this every morning; however, there are times when you and your family may need to leave super early to catch a flight, an early doctor's appointment, or an athletic practice. This trick works for adults too!

Wardrobe and Style

Wardrobe and style choices have the ability to waste gigantic amounts of your time, and money. We keep things incredibly simple and organized in this category of life! I am not willing to waste precious moments with my family picking out outfits and worrying about things that do not matter whatsoever.

Tie Dye

Tie dye any lightly stained clothes to extend their life. Both my kids can ruin an outfit in just moments after putting it on. I have no idea how they do it, but they do. Anything that is worth salvaging, I tie dye. It's much cheaper to tie dye over a small stain than to replace, and much more convenient, too.

Lay Out the Week

We always lay out our kids clothes and outfits for the week ahead. Laying out clothes eliminates so many morning headaches it's not even funny. If your child is a picky dresser or just plain tough in the morning, you can let them pick their pocket for the day. I ordered our weekly clothing organizers online from Lillian Vernon, and they have worked out extremely well. Each of our children has a pocket outfit organizer on the on the back of their bedroom door.

Hang Complete Outfits

Hang complete outfits in your kid's closets. When we don't have any more room in our weekly clothing organizers, I will match complete outfits and hang them up, so they are ready to go.

Wear the Same Thing

Many people who are, and have been successful in this world, wear the same thing every day. A few examples are Albert Einstein, Mark Zuckerberg, and Bill Gates. Steve Jobs was also known to wear the same thing every day. People who wear the same thing have less trivial and meaningless decisions to clutter their brain! I wear the same thing all the time, and I always have the same look. A uniform, consistent look makes life so much easier. Pick something and roll with it.

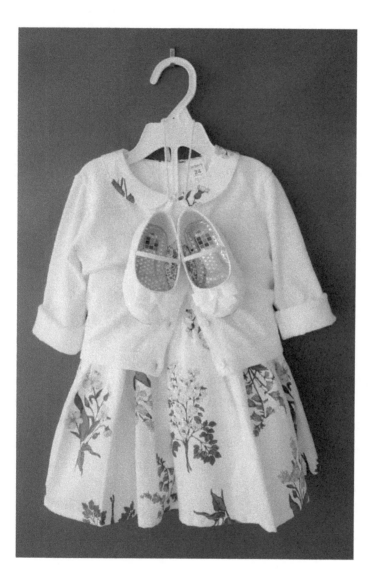

Wear the Same Jewelry

I wear the same set of simple jewelry every single day. I have way too many important decisions to make on a daily basis to worry about jewelry choices. I keep things plain, simple, and easy. Although I am wearing fancy jewelry in the photo on the back of this book, it was not mine. I it borrowed from the photographer.

Always Check for Bugs

I don't care how rushed we are in the morning I always check for bugs while doing my kid's hair. I don't care how rich you are, or what neighborhood you live in; your children will get bugs. I primarily look for lice or ticks. Lice or Lyme Disease from a tick will turn your household completely upside down, which is why you want to detect and eliminate bugs ASAP.

Hang T - Shirts

T- Shirt's end up looking so much nicer and neater when we hang them. It is also so much faster to hang T-shirts than it is to sit and fold them all.

Purchase Like Socks

Try and keep your socks of the same make and model. If you have a million different patterns, it will take so much longer to pair them.

Light Colored Clothing

Be kind to your kids and dress them in all light colors in the summer. This will help prevent them from overheating because light colors reflect light. This also makes it much easier to spot bugs such as a tick or other outdoor bug crawling on your child.

Romper Roll Down

If you have a diarrhea or vomiting crisis with your baby, simply roll down the baby's romper from the top to avoid face contamination. That's actually why the folds are there, so you can pull everything down from the top.

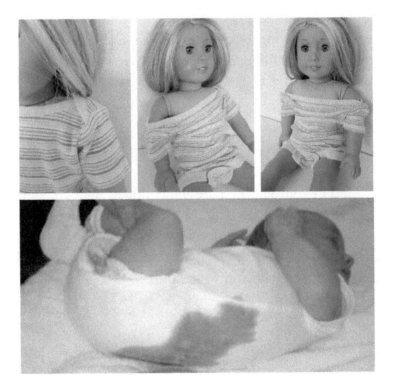

Eliminate Nails

If I have to choose between time with my family, and sitting in a nail salon for over an hour getting my nails done, my family will win every time. Another factor in my decision to eliminate nails is that many times your nails can be an indicator of your overall health. If you cover your nails, you are not able to see if they are dry and cracking, or clear and healthy.

My only exception to this hack is I'm always game for a pedicure splurge. Pedicures are worth every penny and are incredibly relaxing. If I do choose to indulge in a pedicure I skip polish because I do not have time for the upkeep that is involved.

Lotion Hairspray

If you run out of hairspray, lotion works really well to catch fly-away hair and also to keep hair in place. All you need is a tiny pea sized drop of lotion. Rub the lotion in your hands to warm it up and then fix whatever hair is out of place. I would not get into the habit of doing this on a regular basis because lotion will clearly weigh down your hair. Lotion hairspray is perfect in pinch situations.

Plain & Simple Style

I keep everything from my car, makeup, wardrobe and hair, as straightforward and low maintenance as possible. Low maintenance living allows me to focus on much more important issues and priorities in my life.

Photo by Peter Mellekas

Limit Wardrobe

There is no need for each household member to own more than a week's worth of outfits per season. I know some of you are laughing right now but, seriously, that's all you need! Why do we feel the need to jam pack every single closet in our homes?

Buy a Little Larger for Kids

I always purchase our kids' shoes and clothing on the larger side, so they have room to grow, and their clothing lasts longer.

Home Hair Cuts

Home haircuts will save you both time and money. If you are even remotely good with scissors and/or a trimmer you can give your kids haircuts. Taking my kids for haircuts always ends up being a fiasco and an expensive fiasco at that! No thanks!

Get Connected

Who is in your village? Do you have a village? I hope you have a village if you have kids. Your community may consist of family and friends, or just friends, or just family. You need people around you. There is no way in the world that I could exist on this planet without my village. I love them all so dearly. We go through good times and bad times together, and all of it is just awesome.

If you don't have a village, you need to create one. Your kids deserve that! Your village must be the highest quality people that you can possibly surround you and your family with! People that you know will be there no matter what. They will ride with you in both the limo and the broken down bus. Those are your people.

Church

No matter what your faith or religion, find a church and go regularly. Church is an excellent way to meet people and connect. Without God and church in my life, I would be a total mess. There have been times in my life during pregnancy and Lyme Disease that I physically could not attend church, and I would watch it on TV or online. You can actually join churches online now. Online church services are a great and extremely convenient way for housebound people to worship. There is a perfect church out there for everyone. I could not imagine my life without church and God in it! Amen!

Be There for Your Village

Life is a give and take. It goes both ways. I will bend over backward for my village. We are all superhuman for each other, and always go to each other's rescue. I will help these people before I do anything else. They are at the very top of my priority list, and I am at the top of theirs.

Fire Friends

I treat friends, by my own philosophy, like colleagues. I fire, hire, promote and demote. We all do this on a subconscious level. I am more conscious and deliberate about it. If you have kids, there is little to no room for nonsense. If a friend is consistently letting me down or intentionally causing our family added stress or harm, I will fire them. There is usually little recourse just as there is in the business world.

Keep this in mind for family members, too. I usually have a much higher threshold for family members but, that said, I do not let anyone cross our lines and boundaries, no matter who they are.

Hook Up

Hook up with other parents through social media. Most schools have social media pages and group emails. If you haven't jumped into the social media shark tank yet, now is probably the time.

Had I not plugged myself into social media, I would have no idea what's going on. Since I am friends with many parents in the community on social media, we can connect real time for many different reasons. Sometimes it's something simple such as buses are running late, or it may be a discussion about school closing early, carpooling, or sometimes it's all three. These social media pages are amazing tools that we have right at our disposal. Because of social media, I can stay up to date with news and community events through the quick touch of my cell phone.

Whatever you do, don't overindulge on social media. Social media can be extremely unproductive and negative if you allow it to be! Seriously limit your time on social media pages.

Use Internet Connect Sites

Use the internet to connect with the world. The internet allows us to meet a mate, or perhaps a neighbor to play cards with. There are so many amazing connect sites out there. You can find meet up groups for just about every make and model out there. If you have a computer there is no reason that you should not be able to plug into your state, town, neighborhood, local hobby interest groups, medical community groups and the list goes on.

Trade Favors

Trade favors and barter with other parents when you can. This is a win-win for all, including your community.

Shopping

Who else loathes shopping? I used to like shopping before I had kids. Now it's a dreadful, time-sucking chore that I am responsible for. Anything that can make shopping easier is a win in my book.

Order Online

Order as much as humanly possible online. Being a busy parent is survival of the fittest. If I can have someone deliver all needed household items, I am not going to argue with that. Most websites offer free shipping and I end up spending less money shopping online. We order everything from toilet paper, diapers, wipes, water jugs, clothing, school supplies, groceries, and everything else that we can online. We support local business whenever possible. Our groceries are ordered online and delivered from a local grocery store.

Don't forget to use a coupon code every single time you make an online purchase. Not looking for a coupon code is like throwing money in the garbage. Take the two extra seconds and find a code!

Small Stores

If you need just one quick thing, go to the smallest store possible, so you are in and out. We have a local store in Rhode Island called Benny's. It has everything you need, and the store is small so that you can get in and out quickly. There is rarely a line or wait.

Buy and Sell Online

We buy and sell gently used household items online all the time. Internet thrifting is a fantastic asset to any home. I don't know how I would get rid of half the junk that we acquire if not for internet thrifting. There is nothing like one of your kids wearing a $50 pair of sneakers once, and never wearing them again. All of that goes online.

Dollar Tree

I have lived off The Dollar Tree at many different points in my life. From groceries to toys, books, and other fun items, everything is a dollar. I used to treat my son Jack to a Dollar Tree 'shopping spree' when he was little. We were so broke at that time.

The Dollar Tree allowed me to do some pretty cool stuff with Jack at a very financially low point in my life. I still shop there and I still love it! The Dollar Tree is also nice because there is no temptation to splurge and, if you do, the damage is minimal.

Reusable Grocery Bags

I think plastic bags should be outlawed, but that's just me. Both my husband and I use a set of durable, reusable grocery bags while shopping. Our bags are way more durable and convenient for hauling items home from the store, if we physically go to the store. If I do end up with a plastic bag from a store, it's usually terrible and rips, so I never forget my bags.

Measure with Twine

Stretch a piece of twine the length of your child's garment or shoe, then cut a piece to the desired length for shopping. This trick allows you to shop without your child having to try things on. Doing this allows you to get a size ballpark.

You can also cut a piece of twine to the exact size of your child's foot, or inseam. This avoids having to drag your child around to different stores.

Farmers Markets

Shop local farmers markets for fresh produce and crafts from artists and farmers. We enjoy visiting local farmers markets as a family. There is always something exciting going on for kids such as goat and chick visits, book readings, bands, and more. We enjoy the experience of shopping and getting fresh air and exercise at the same time.

Thrift Stores

Thrift stores are amazing as long as you are not a hoarder. Thrifting is great for the planet, and for everyone who does it.

I have bought both Jack and Katie way more things than I care to admit at thrift stores. Perfect prices and perfect for our planet. Everything about thrifting is perfect.

Coupon and Receipt Boxes

Make two small separate boxes to store receipts and coupons. Both of these items can make a real mess out of your living space or your office. Keeping an efficient and up to date box of receipts for every single thing that you spend money on can help with filing taxes, making a return, budgeting and more!

I keep coupons in their own box because I could never find a coupon when I needed one before this system was in place. We would put them in random spots and drawers around our home. Now everything is right where it should be.

Activities

Activities with kids are never ending.

Kids are forever on the fly and need constant entertainment. This chapter contains some of our very favorite activities to do as a busy modern family.

Shipping Box Crafts

Cut shipping boxes from internet purchases to make amazing free craft canvases. I cut shipping cardboard into perfect squares, and our kids go crazy coloring, painting, and gluing things to them! You don't need a fancy new white canvas from a craft store; light brown cardboard works just fine! When our kids finish their project, we simply stack cardboard projects for storage.

Occasionally I will spray paint a bunch of cut cardboard squares white to mix things up. I also use cut pieces of shipping cardboard to mount and 'frame' school art projects. If we professionally framed every school project that came home, we would be homeless. I also mount completed puzzles on shipping cardboard, and they turn out looking really nice. Cardboard crafts are also fantastic for school classrooms because the cost is minimal, if not free.

Lucky Penny

Teach your kids to look for lucky pennies with you. Picking up lucky pennies is an excellent way to teach children the value of money. My entire little family gets excited when one of us finds a lucky penny. We always look at the year and discuss the era that penny was created. This activity is something my kids will remember forever. It costs nothing and is so much fun. My kids love putting lucky pennies in their piggy banks too. Always be safe if you are looking in parking lots.

Activity Bags

Have a designated bag for each activity that your child participates. Put everything relating to that activity in that bag. After items for all sports and activities come out of the laundry, return it directly to the appropriate bag. Activity bags are the only way that we remain organized and sane with multiple activities going on simultaneously within our home.

Custom Coloring Sheets

Custom-made coloring sheets are a great activity for events and parties. Printable custom coloring sheets are incredibly cheap to have made online. I usually pay just a couple of dollars for a custom template and then print as many as I need. I have ordered these in the past for Valentine's Day cards for my children to take to school.

If you look online, you can find all sorts of themes and templates to choose from for your kid's birthday parties and other special events. Adults and children both usually enjoy custom coloring pages.

Life Jacket

Keep a life jacket in your car during warmer months. If you have a child who does not know how to swim yet, throw a life jacket on them any time you are going to be near water. It only takes a few seconds for tragedies to happen. A child drowning because they are not wearing a life jacket near a swimming pool, lake, or other body of water, is an avoidable situation.

Vintage Plasticware with Lids

One of my favorite finds at thrift stores are old plastic servers with dividers and lids. I use these servers for crafting, and other household projects. Plasticware lids also double as a crafting workstation tray.

If you can find a plastic server with a lid, that's a score! Vintage plasticware pieces are not PBA free so do not cook with them, or heat them up. We use them just for crafting fun.

Hang Arts and Crafts

Use a coat hanger and clothes pins to hang art for drying or for display. You can nail a small nail into a wall and hang the coat hanger on it to show off projects. This works for school classrooms and the workplace too. You can also nail up a twine clothesline and use clothes pins to display photos, birthday and holiday cards, artwork and other items. It's a neat 'look' and moves clutter and mess out of your way and somewhere that can it can also be enjoyed.

Search

Search for something that is widespread in nature where you live. Do you have interesting rocks, acorns or sand? Rhode Island offers some of the most beautiful beaches in the country, with an endless supply of tumbled stones, sea glass and shells.

When we have free time, we love searching for sea glass on our beach shores. We take a bucket on our adventures and collect all different colors and sizes of sea glass. We often make crafts out of our sea glass, which is all completely free. Quality-based activities are paramount to our family.

YMCA

Any family regardless of income or financial status can become a member of the YMCA. The YMCA provides affordable lessons for kids; free babysitting while you exercise in most locations, community events, affordable before- and after-school care, recreational play rooms, parties and so much more. If you have not checked out your local YMCA, you are missing out! We love our YMCA!

Join the Library

The library is not what it used to be. Now in most cases, you can order books, movies and other items right from your phone and have them delivered to your nearest library! That's crazy! It's all free! The library also has phenomenal free enrichment classes for both kids and adults. Our local library has occasional baby duck visits, free museum passes, movie nights, craft hours, conference rooms and more.

Movies

We don't take our kids to the movie theater anymore. It's that simple. We rent most of our movies through our cable company. We took both of our children to the movie theater a few times. You know where I am going with this. One pooped in their diaper when we arrived, and the other one wanted to go for a walk! That's my version of pure torture. Not for the prices that movie theaters are charging now either. For a small family to go to the movies, it's almost triple digits including drinks and popcorn, which is outrageous. Who can afford that?

We set up our own movie situation at home. We get comfy, turn the lights off, and our kids love it. We buy a small amount of candy, popcorn and other goodies at the grocery store so we all feel like we are getting a special treat. This whole concept has worked out well. If someone has to go potty or get more water, you know the deal, it goes on and on, we are at home and can accommodate everyone's needs.

Driveway Parking

If you let your kids play in your driveway, park at the end, so they are not able to ride off on their bikes or escape. Create a blockade. Even if my kids can ride around and access the street, this creates a mental barrier for my kids, and they won't travel past it. We do this as an extra safety cushion, even when we are outside with our children, as we always are.

Lemonade Stand

Create a lemonade stand with your child. You can get creative and fun. We do this with our kids every summer to raise money for different local causes and charities, and they love it. Our children learn about business and giving to an important cause, and we all have a blast while doing it!

Write a Letter

If your children require sponsorship funds for any type of activity, consider writing a letter like this one. We loved receiving this letter and, yes, this young lady received a sponsorship check from the Cornell Family.

I adore Brooke's photo on the bottom right of this sponsorship request letter. This hack can be applied to any sport or activity. It's professional, classy, and conveys all information in an efficient manor.

Internet fundraising accounts are fabulous as well and better for the environment, however not everyone has a computer which is occasionally the case with Grandparents and other various family members. This fancy letter would be perfect to give to a boss or other special members of your village. I love it.

January 31, 2017

Dear Friend,

Thank you for your interest in sponsoring my participation in the Miss New Hampshire Pageant this April. I'm excited to be competing for my first time at the "miss" level! Who knows, maybe I'll be crowned in September as Miss America 2018!

I hold the local title of Miss Weirs Beach, and have already earned over $5,500 in scholarships to the college of my choice. Currently I am a student at the New Hampshire Technical Institute completing pre-chiropractic coursework, which is similar to a pre-med program.

There are several ways you can support my participation:

- Place an ad in our program book. This full color souvenir book is distributed free to every ticket holder. Thousands of people will see your ad (¼ page is $75; ½ page is $125; Full page is $250) Our ad deadline is February 15th!
- Make a donation to my CMN fund ($250 total donations are required to be a contestant in the state pageant) Go to: http://www.missamericaforkids.org/Donate/BrookeMills
- Donate an item or a gift certificate for our Miss NH Ball silent auction
- Make a monetary donation to help defray the cost of my wardrobe and talent preparations
- Purchase a "Miss NH Ball raffle calendar" for $10 from me for a chance to win gift cards or $200 cash

Thank you so much for your consideration and willingness to help! I'm excited about the opportunities that are ahead! Donations can be mailed to:

Brooke Mills

Concord, New Hampshire 03301

Sincerely,

♥ Brooke

Brooke Mills

Miss Weirs Beach

Photo credit: Jenn Cady

Big Box Craft Classes

We attend dozens of free craft classes at various stores that host them. You can find a free kids class at most hardware, craft, and even some grocery stores. Take advantage of what the area around you has to offer. We always try and give these stores business when we can because they are so good to our kids and our community!

Egg Carton Crafts

We upcycle empty plastic egg carton containers. I wash containers out with hot water and soap before we use them for crafts. Do not wash them in the dishwasher because they will melt. We use empty egg cartons to sort rocks, beads, jewels, and as paint dipping stations. These crates are also perfect for displaying Easter egg creations; simply cut the lid off with scissors and the crate becomes an egg display case!

Summer at McDonald's

I know this goes against everything I usually say, but we adore splurging on McDonalds at the beginning of each summer. We love getting the special toys that they put in their summer happy meals. You can buy just the toy for a couple of dollars; you do not have to buy the entire happy meal, although they are extremely affordable.

For the past three summers we have collected the entire Minions Collection, Secret Life of Pets Collection, and this summer we are collecting Beenie Boos. Again I know this one activity goes against everything that I advise but the toys are small, the happy meals are cheap and for whatever the reason the summer toys rock. This is one of our favorite family traditions!

Be Healthy

In order to survive any type of grind, you and your family need to be as healthy as possible. We have certain things that keep us healthy that are nonnegotiable. We do these things most of the time. I say most of the time because nobody is perfect when it comes to diet and nutrition! Do your best!

Water

What can I say? We drink a ton of water in our house, all of us. Large amounts of water is a must-do for everyone. If you still drink from individual plastic bottles in your home, label the caps of all bottles with a small sticker or marker so the 'unknown opened' do not get wasted.

Vitamin Baskets

I created household 'yes' 'no' baskets, so we all remember to take our vitamins. All of our vitamins start the day in the 'no' basket, then as we take them, they make their way to the 'yes' basket. Baskets are an easy way to keep track of who has taken their vitamins and who has not. This method also works for households with special needs members who take sizable amounts of meds. I keep a tiny printed calendar next to our baskets to check off each day that I move our vitamins from 'no' to 'yes'.

Bone Broth

This soup works like magic on immune systems. We learned about bone broth during the height of my battle with Lyme Disease. Now we make it on a regular basis and add kale, carrots, and chicken chunks. This soup packs serious healing power. Research it!

Minimize Caffeine & Sugar

It's impossible to eliminate these completely. Reducing to a bare minimum is necessary for optimal health. Period.

Supplements

Everyone in our home takes vitamins and supplements. We also take probiotics, and a multi-vitamin to keep our immune systems healthy and robust. Food that is available in this modern world is so completely void of nutrition. If you do not take vitamins and supplements there is no way that you or your family are meeting your daily nutritional requirements.

Exercise

If you don't exercise, your health will eventually fall apart. Every part of your body benefits positively from a light exercise. Figure it out. You have to do it.

PJ Gym Clothes

Sleep in your gym clothes if you have a hard time motivating in the morning. You will be more likely to make it to the gym if you are already dressed for it.

Cover Mattresses

We cover all mattresses in our house with allergy barrier covers. It might be a coincidence, but our family gets sick much less often since we started using mattress covers. Dust mites and dust can be embedded in your mattress without you even knowing it. Anything that reduces annoying colds and illnesses for our family is a no brainer for me.

Belly Band

Wear a belly band after childbirth. It will place all of your stomach muscles back where they need to be. I wore one after I had both of my kids. It was amazing what it did for back pain and my stomach. I wish hospitals would give one to every new mom post-birth.

Organic Vitamin C Lollipops

I give c pops to my kids in the winter. They are organic lollies that are packed with vitamin c to give immune systems a boost. You can find them online or at your local natural foods store.

Take a Hot Bath

Taking a hot bath or shower will almost always make me feel better. A warm bath will sometimes even calm a super cranky baby. I used to do this with Jack all of the time when he was little.

Space Vaccines

I spaced out all of my children's vaccines. Both are up to date and current on all their vaccines; however, when it came to vaccines I did not mess around with either one of my kids. Yes there is a thing called vaccine injury and yes it is real. This is how I handled vaccines for my kids,

- Two shots max per doctor's visit, one shot if it was a 'three in one' special.

- Vaccines visits had to be administered at least one month apart from each other.

- My kids were not allowed any shots if they were sick what so ever. My pediatrician would say 'but Mrs. Cornell you're going to have to pay a few extra co-pays for additional shot visits!' Um ok, I'm good with that!

I always wonder what happens when a child gets loaded with a bunch of vaccines at once, and then has a severe allergic reaction, how does anyone know which one caused the reaction? It's a slippery slope people.

Do your research parents.

Record Folders

Keep folders of medical records and blood lab results for every member of your family. MD's are extremely busy. Doctors do not have time to study all of your medical records. Keeping track of your child's medical records is your job as a parent. Maintain records in chronological order.

Keeping records might seem a little extreme, but it helps avoid wasting valuable time with doctors and provides all involved with a better snapshot of what is going on. If you have a disabled or chronically ill family member, this hack is extremely beneficial.

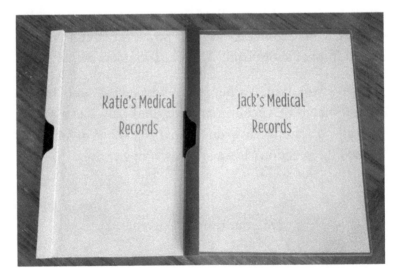

Fancy Toothbrush

A sure way to get your kids to brush their teeth is if they like their toothbrush. Automatic battery-operated toothbrushes work well for my kids. You can also score some pretty awesome toothbrushes from The Dollar Tree. I use fancy toothbrushes as rewards from Santa, The Easter Bunny, and The Tooth Fairy. Doing this makes toothbrushes and teeth brushing glamorous for your kids.

Sleep

You need it. Everyone needs sleep. You have to get enough sleep. Lack of sleep will cause a serious crash and burn. Your growing kids also need plenty of sleep. Make sufficient sleep an important part of your household and routine.

Fairy Tales

One of my children came home with head lice once. It was catastrophic to our household. It's in all the schools-public and private. It's everywhere. Lice should be covered by homeowners insurance. Talk about turning our house upside-down. It's like having mold or smoke damage. Every little thing in our house had to be cleaned and sanitized, every piece of cloth had to be washed, or steam cleaned. All area rugs needed to be cleaned; I mean its big time. I hope we never have to go through that again!

I was upset during our previous lice situation when one of my friends told me about Fairy Tales Shampoo. Fairytale products are made with gentle and child safe ingredients, and most bugs hate it including lice and even other bugs. This is all the stuff that seriously no one tells you when you become a parent! We have used Fairy Tales for almost two years now, and it's awesome! No bugs! We use the entire line of products, including the body wash.

Avon Skin So Soft body wash is also a favorite of ours. Jack really likes the smell, and it's another fantastic bug repellent.

Doctor's Appts on Speaker

If you have a particular health issue or concern, information that we learn at doctor appointments can be precious. If one parent or guardian is unable to attend an important doctor visit for your child, do the visit on speaker. Speaker calls save a tremendous amount of time, especially for divorced parents. Doing this allows everyone to be on the same page automatically without any subsequent or redundant communications.

Say No to Everything

What does this have to do with your health? If you run yourself ragged, you will be useless to yourself, your family, your responsibilities, and to the world. We say no to most invitations. We do nothing out of pressure or obligation. If our family truly wants to do something we do it, otherwise we relax. Some of our most amazing family moments are just hanging out in our living room as a family, playing games and enjoying each other's company.

Tech Time

Technology is a godsend for parents. Technology allows us to accomplish great things and work smarter. If you are not using your readily available technology, you are wasting valuable tools that could be a game changer for you and your family!

Car Remote Safety

Before we installed our home alarm system, I would keep our car keys by our bed. Your car alarm has a panic button on it that you can press in an emergency situation. Intruders will not want to mess with you or your family with sirens blasting outside your home. This works for health emergencies, too. I also use the panic button of my car alarm system to find my car in large parking lots. It works every single time.

Robot Assistants

Use as many robots in your home as you can. Some of my favorite robot assistants are robot vacuum cleaners, Alexa from Amazon, and Siri on my cell phone. I have Siri do math for me all the time when I am crunching numbers at work or home. Some robots are like having a human assistant. Most are completely worth the money.

Screen Time

I limit all screen time. My kids love electronics just like most do. I save screen times for special occasions and as a reward for good behavior. If you allow frequent screen time, then it loses its effect and won't work in a stressful situation such as a long car ride, airplane flight or doctor's appointment.

Research

I research every single little thing. Why not? We all have the information superhighway right at our fingertips. We would be crazy not to utilize the internet for research. The internet is a free assistant for me. If you become skilled at internet researching, you can use it in many aspects of your life.

Online Videos

You and your children can learn how to do just about anything on the internet. My son took it upon himself to learn how to tie his shoes online. It's amazing what types of informational videos are out there and most are free. Take advantage of them!

Security System

Install the best security system that you can afford. You can easily set your house or apartment up with cameras, voice notification when doors and windows open, remote surveillance from your phone and more. We know every time a child opens a door or window and we can visually monitor what's going on at our home remotely.

Home security is a no brainer especially with how affordable it's become. Most major retailers sell DIY home security systems for those who are even slightly tech savvy. You can get as fancy as you want with some of the newer DIY security systems. A few of my friends have doorbells with cameras. Doorbell cameras take photos when they sense movement or activity.

Cell Phone

One can run an entire company or household from a cell phone. We all pay dearly per month for our cell phones, and we should be using all the different features that they have to offer. With just one smartphone you can:

1. Use it as a level
2. Shop
3. Use it as a flashlight
4. Check sports scores
5. Use it as a white noise machine for babies
6. Buy and sell online
7. Use it for a video conference with your boss or kids while your away
8. Use it as a coupon finder while shopping in stores
9. Use it as a book
10. Surf the internet
11. Use it as a calculator
12. Use Siri or Ask Google as a personal assistant
13. Use it as a talking map
14. Check your email
15. Send a text message
16. Make a 'to do' list
17. Order library books
18. Use it as a video recorder
19. Check the weather

20. Use it as a documenting device. If your kids get a rash, take a photo, and then it's documented, along with a date and time stamp. How many times do you go to the pediatrician and forget all important facts! Take random photos of your check-in's. I never remember when I was where, but my cell phone helps remind me.

21. Replace your camera with it. I photographed and edited this entire book with my cell phone.

22. Set up reminders

23. Watch a movie

24. Edit, view and print your internet calendar

25. Use it as a voice recorder for work meetings.

26. Operate your home alarm system remotely and view any surveillance cameras.

27. Monitor social media

28. Download educational games for your kids

29. Listen to music

30. Make business transactions through Square

31. Use it as an alarm clock

32. Listen to the radio

33. Print pictures right from your phone onto your home printer

34. Look up recipes on the fly

35. Download coloring apps for your kids

36. Dictate notes, emails, and messages
37. Find the nearest gas station
38. Set up speaker phone
39. Get emergency alerts
40. Compare local gas prices
41. Read the news
42. Check on stock prices
43. Monitor your teenager's speed while they are driving and receive a text message when they go over a certain speed.
44. Receive text messages when your children depart and arrive at intended destinations
45. Count calories
46. Receive daily motivational quotes and bible verses
47. Use home school apps
48. Complete homework
49. Set up a Go Fund Me for a friend
50. Install a phone locator, so your phone can always be found no matter what.
51. Check on hunting, fishing, sailing, beach and lake conditions.
52. Find mixed drink recipes
53. Use it as a language translator through Google
54. Operate lights within your home
55. Operate your slow cooker from work

This list is just the tip of the iceberg with all that you can do with your phone. All of us have this amazing technology right at our fingertips! I do not use the technology on my phone enough!

Social Media

Use social media to your advantage. Follow all of your children's favorite local attractions to stay connected. I follow anything pertaining to my state, my town, our schools, and similar news and events. I really would have no idea what's going on if it weren't for social media. I am able to see what local kids events are happening in my town through this medium. It's really fantastic.

Take social media breaks. Check out and clear your mind for a few days! Social media can become extremely toxic and unhealthy. I don't like to spend a sizable amount of time on social media under any circumstance.

Conclusion

In conclusion, I think we can all see a few common themes in this book. A few lessons that really stick out are:

Minimalism, Preparation, and Technology

In order to win at parenting as a busy parent, you must somehow find a way to simplify and minimalize your entire life, you must be and stay prepared, and you most certainly must take advantage of the technology that is available to all of us in this modern age.

Life is a marathon, not a sprint. If you fall, get right back up and try again. It may take you years to set up your ideal, smooth household and life. Start today and try something new each day to get you and your family one step closer to where you want to be. If you don't try, you will never win!